Flight Risk

Flight Risk

Poems and Translations by

DB Jonas

© 2025 DB Jonas. All rights reserved.
This material may not be reproduced in any form, published,
reprinted, recorded, performed, broadcast,
rewritten, or redistributed without
the explicit permission of DB Jonas.
All such actions are strictly prohibited by law.

Cover design by Shay Culligan
Cover image: Joseph Cornell *Owl Box, 1945-46* ©
The Joseph and Robert Cornell Memorial Foundation /
Licensed by VAGA at Artists Rights Society (ARS), NY
Cover photo courtesy Art Resource: Digital Image ©
CNAC/MNAM, Dist. RMN-Grand Palais / Art Resource, NY
Author photo by Juliana Carlson

ISBN: 978-1-63980-681-2

Kelsay Books
502 South 1040 East, A-119
American Fork, Utah 84003
Kelsaybooks.com

for Julie

Who brought us world enough and time

Acknowledgments

The following poems first appeared in these journals:

The Amphibian: "Georgics in a Plague Year," "Genealogies"
arc 30, Journal of the Israel Association of Writers in English: "The Bonds of Separation" (as "Flesh and Bone")
Cathexis Northwest: "Flight Risk," "The Laureate"
The Chained Muse: Petrarch's "Or che 'l ciel," "I dolci colli," "Gli occhi di ch'io parlai," "Ite, rime dolente;" "After Francisco de Quevedo," "After Maurice Scève," "After Eugenio Montale, Meriggiare," "After Yves Bonnefoy, Aux Arbres," "After Valéry, His Palme" (translations)
The Deronda Review: "After Moshe ibn Ezra" (translation)
The Ekphrastic Review: "Klee at Carthage"
The Galway Review: "His Difficulties," "Emblems of Alterity," "Physics 101," "Scissiparity," "Visitations of Spring," "Of Time and Weather," "As Gravity Builds Bone," "Anamneses," "Pastoral," "Tristes Tropiques," "Ainadamar," "Not the Landscape," "Gertrude to Her Chambermaid," "Present at the Dawn of Creation"
Jerry Jazz Musician: "Wrong Address"
Merion West: "Amnesia Palace," "This Excess Our Sentience," "Following Bishop"
The New Lyre: "The Familiar" (as "Leaving Babylon"), "Smashing Atoms with a Hammer," "The Dragons of Paradise," "Twilight of the Idols"
New Mexico State Poetry Society Anthology 2023 (Glissando!): "Sgraffito"
The Orchards Poetry Journal: "Instructions for the Memoirist"
Snatches of an Aria (Pure Slush Books): "Cocktails with the Critic"
Tar River Poetry: "The Sisyphus of Demolition"

Contents

I

Flight Risk	15
Amnesia Palace	16
Following Bishop	18
His Difficulties	19
Tristes Tropiques	20
Ainadamar	22
Letter to an Unborn Poet	24
The Laureate	26

II

Klee at Carthage	29
Celestial Motion	30
Verisimilitude	31
Of Time and Weather	33
Scissiparity	34
This Excess Our Sentience	35
Among the Obstinate Nostalgias	37
Emblems of Alterity	38
In Finitude	39
Street People	42
The Gaze of Another	47
Incompletion Ode	52

III

Visitations of Spring	55
Volunteers	56
Eos	58
Flyfishing	59

As Gravity Builds Bone	60
Jellyman	61
Physics 101	62
Absent at the Dawn of Creation	65
Georgics in a Plague Year	67
Pastoral	69
The Dragons of Paradise	70
The Sisyphus of Demolition	75

IV

Sgraffito	79
The Bonds of Separation	81
Genealogies	83
Instructions for the Memoirist	86
Smashing Atoms with a Hammer	88
All Knowledge Is Carnal	89
Not the Landscape	91
Anamneses	92

V

A Note to Hrotsvit	97
Cocktails with the Critic	99
His Treason	103
Gertrude to Her Chambermaid	105
Wrong Address	107
The Majordomo and the Kibbutznik	109

VI

Twilight of the Idols	115
The Familiar	118
11.8.2016	122

VII

De deserto clamavi: An Introduction to the Translations	127
After Hanagid, His *Ruined Citadel*	128
After Moshe Ibn Ezra	129
Francesco Petrarca: Or che 'l ciel e la terra e 'l vento tace	131
Francesco Petrarca: I dolci colli ov'io lasciai me stesso	132
Francesco Petrarca: Gli occhi di ch'io parlai sí caldamente	133
Francesco Petrarca: Ite, rime dolente, al duro sasso	134
After Francisco De Quevedo	135
Maurice Scève: Le Jour Passé De Ta Doulce Presence	136
After Paul Valéry, His *Palme*	137
After Yves Bonnefoy, *Aux Arbres*	140
After Eugenio Montale, *Meriggiare*	141

I

So we beat on, boats against the current, borne back ceaselessly into the past.

—F. Scott Fitzgerald, *The Great Gatsby*

Flight Risk

on a Joseph Cornell Owl

She occupies a mental space
reserved for disappearances.
In your mind's eye, she's only
barely there. In hers, you're
something that has never been.

Her dark regard's a one-way
street; this ice-blue reverie's
her native element. Her talons
grasp the night she gazes on,
an iron grip devoid of sentiment.

Your limping stanzas try to own
the fierce poetics of her stare,
to seize the silences you think
you hear. Although in silence
she's already flown, her absence
doesn't leave your thought alone.

Amnesia Palace

People fix in their minds places of the greatest possible extent . . . such as a large house, divided into many apartments.
　　　　　—Quintilian, *Institutio Oratoria*

Out of nowhere, a stiffening breeze.
He opened his eyes.
The far shore wore a gauzy veil of rain.
Thunderheads towered over Evian
and shook the silver surface of the lake,
ruffling like shot silk.

Below his narrow seat down at the quay,
along the little inlet, black swans drifted,
dozing unperturbed in the rising chop.
All the canvas chairs around him
billowed out and wildly flapped,
and made an irritated, snapping sound.

He closed his eyes again. The odors
of the old hotel behind him coiled
in his nostril. Beneath his shuttered lids,
the tattered draperies, the derelict galleries,
the once-grand frescoes of this frowzy,
threadbare refuge out of season.

Drifting in the soft spray
of the approaching storm, he wandered
in and out, it seemed, through the musty
corridors of habitude and arbitrary revery,
past empty niches of the mind lined up
along the winding walls of indirection.

Unruly grammars slid like sleek ball bearings
beneath the archings of his vaulted palate,
sailed like planets in their deathless transit,
skittered and collided like billiards arrayed
upon the green baize surfaces of memory,
rolled like tapioca on the tongue.

***

Once the squall had passed,
the bellman ambled down the hill
to fetch him up for tea,
this solitary pensioner, living relic
of the old school, whose thickset
poems posed such intractable difficulties
for the unsuspecting reader.

Startling to his name, he awakened slowly
into the shafted light. The redolent
melodies of dreaming lingered, ringing
in his anxious ear, while all the blithe,
unruffled swans, awake, erect and gliding
in the autumn dusk, darkly bobbed
and swayed like omens brooding
on the mirrored lake.

Following Bishop

Come follow, if you choose, the clacking heel,
the slender foot, the measured step,

the darkening tide, the silvery shingled shore,
the heavy, mirthful scent of orchids in the air.

Come sit beside the coiling nimbus of her cigarette
to examine these disjecta from the chambered sea

beneath the callous sky's fluorescent, glaucus light,
and witness all these prodigies of cruelty and lust,

the mournful slap of wavelets on a littered beach,
these sambas made from common speech, her sly

exactitudes all primly buttoned at the throat. Behold
the buoyed continents by color rearranged, a shy

insistence in your ear, the voice of daylight dread,
of soft sonorities that bring the farthest things up close.

His Difficulties

He held the world a knowable thing. Thoughts,
the greater mysteries, sailing in and out of view,
swooped and skimmed like swallows in the eaves.

An orchard orbited beneath his purpling sky.
There is in all this alien noise, he knew,
a grim, remorseless striving to be understood,

a ruthlessness alert in the arresting hand,
some ingenuity required to occupy the listener's
least attentive ear, her disembodied breath,

to penetrate the cool indifference images provoke,
arouse the aimless concentration sounds require,
insinuate the mortal difference meanings make.

He channeled all this swirling tide of indirection
through the ragged cutbanks of the intellect,
pruned back the infinite allusiveness that poems are,

and redirected oceans past familiar stands
of hornbeam, birch and sycamore to populate
his vast disorienting landscapes with familiar sights,

horizons for the sure dead-reckoning they'd need
to navigate the fleet frivolity of thought, negotiate
his obdurate, intractable, his irreducible difficulties.

Tristes Tropiques

on Stevens

It is always daybreak there. The slant light,
        the back-lit leaf, the saline breath
of tropic trade-wind on the skin. Autumns,
        present and departed, fixed in amber.

Past master of the *à propos,* he manufactures
        arias that fracture on arrival,
the fragrance of lost things, their lingering, the ornate
        silver, each heirloom salver of desiring.

What unprecedented idioms arise and shatter
        on the substance of the insubstantial!
What images of all that managed to escape attention,
        what startled lexicons of dispossession!

Ice sculptures sail like swans upon the mind.
        He's left this mirrored trail of ice behind,
lapidary in the lifting light. We're left to navigate
        the crystalline flotillas of his thought.

You'd think he'd put our overheated rhetoric to bed
        for good, but no, since poems
surface only from the powerless in things,
        the impersonal, the inconsequential.

So think on it, if you're so inclined. Just what is it
        we expect from poets now?
Chronicles of indignation? outrage? gross injustice?
        Canticles of feeling deeply felt?

If so, his works are doomed to disappear in time,
    to deliquesce like swans of ice at noon,
but this Spinoza of our climate met his passion
    in the coolest mornings of the intellect,

in the soundscapes of desire, in vocabularies
    that predate thought, predate indignation,
to invoke the vulgates of a distant weather,
    auguries of other Autumns, other Springs.

It seems it's always morning there. A slant light
    without irony. Leaves tremble softly
in the air. Otherwise, his imperfect world lies still,
    effulgent, cocooned as if in amber.

Ainadamar*

Sometime in the early hours, he realized that calm
had filled the trembling space where dread had been,
and in the deafening din of locusts through the pines,
along this hillside somewhere over Ainadamar, recognized
the strange relief that only utter hopelessness can bring.

His poet's skin received the strident music bodies made,
creation's brutal, skittering oscillation, felt it escalate across
the wooded valley, upward through the canyon walls that rose
around the tiny villages below, to ignite the atmosphere
and set the colonies of rock and pyrophoric pine aflame.

I saw myself a fashioner of unexpected images, he thought,
of bright unlikelihoods that lived already in the reader's mind
and occupied her reason like recurring dream, but what emerged
instead was always something carnal, epidermal, lubricious,
sounds in rude licentious contact with each other, and with me.

Before the dawning image, before the mind's awakened names,
it was the clarion vowel, the quiet consonant's percussion,
I know now, that had inspired each song and left no choice
but chance to dance upon the page, to lead the hand through
trackless forests of imagining, the senseless noise of meaning.

And the urgent, swarming music of those insect bodies now,
their unmodulated frequencies, called up for him the way that
melodies adrift within the mind inspired the fissile products
of his craft, the way the beckoning world proposed itself to him
as fracture, as abandon, as lurid spectacle and fleeting beauty.

So perhaps there is some sense in all this after all,
this specific body's senseless martyrdom to time and history,
the injustices that lead us where they may, into this specific
cooling shade, this blazing furnace of a buzzing afternoon,
where life's unmerited, untimely leaden gift awaits us all.

From somewhere high above the village street, a sharp report
of rifle-shot unsettled the communal air. Briefly, the bustling
marketplace went silent, and briefly all the locusts seemed
to hold their breath. Then softly, bit by bit, the living murmurs
rose again, into lofty senselessness, into indifference, into life.

---

* In August of 1936, the poet Francisco García Lorca was apprehended by Phalangists in Granada. Two days later he was executed, along with others, on a hillside above the reservoir Ainadamar, The Fountain of Tears. When asked by his friends why he was being apprehended, his captors replied, *"Sus obras:"* *"His works."*

Letter to an Unborn Poet

They seem always to be saying how a danger slumbers
in the slippery word and coils within the simplest speech
to poison thinking with an ever-present dream of Presence,
that evasive insubstantial Manifest that authorizes Essence.

The experts say we must at every cost avoid the soft
nefarious noise of inauthentic talk, the yammering naivetés
of idle chat, the unexamined language of the marketplace,
of honeyed blandishments, of commerce, cant and *idéologie*.

They'll find it all for us, if we but ask, within the glib vocabularies
of our thought, our clueless choice of certain loaded enthymemes,
our battery of commonplace and simile and syllogism,
the way each eager speaking act undoes its own intention.

Yet in poesy they claim to find an exit from this muddle,
a spooky way of being-in-the-world that's neither here nor there,
a sly and playful place where we give reign to sound and fury,
where language runs amok along the mirrored halls of irony.

A poem is but a ludic space, the subtle critic seems to say,
where every utterance invites entanglement in the fissile logic
of the words, abandons blind obeisance to the shadow-play
of meaning in this funhouse-mirrored world of ours, this Real.

Such is the coinage of our realm, it seems, whose obverse face
is the tale of full disclosure, the fawning modesty that bids us
stick to "only what we know," the imprimatur of Authenticity,
to share an incandescent, private fact and hope that fact is pretty.

But what if speech, all speech, occurs outside the cans and cannots
of our viable, voluble world? out past the canons of the possible,
of what it is that can be said and what can not, beyond the thought,
beyond the fact, where truth and lie will never have the final word?

And what if, speaking from beyond the realm of fact itself,
the poem only ever says much more than it can possibly say?
What if it is not a clearing in the wood at all, but a road away
from every place, a road we travel on but can't just up and walk?

If so then, ah, The Authentic, let's just say, for grins, for fun,
for once, for real: what a useless bloody crock!

The Laureate

*The deepening need for words . . . makes us search
the sound of them for a finality, a perfection,
an unalterable vibration.*
   —Wallace Stevens, *The Noble Rider and the Sound of Words*

I turned the volume of his meanings down
in fun one summer afternoon, the way
we'll hope to read in countenance and gesture,
undistracted by the blandishments of voice,
the silent evidence of decency and candor
in the body-language of a politician's pitch.

It was some compelling frequency in his sonorities,
his vibrations, I was after, but for the life of me,
found no peculiar wavelengths there, or startling
evidence of song, no dispatch from the border-
lands of singing's native soil, no news fit
to print beside the earnest dronings of sincerity.

In all that dogged diligence of type there had to be
some urgent riff at work, I figured, an audacious
logic in the line-breaks and happy happenstance
of sly adjacencies, some driving impetus for words
arranged just so upon the page, for that deathless
sound we seek, a noble rider's hoofbeat on the road.

II

*We are water, earth, light and air contracted,
not only before recognizing or representing them,
but before sensing them.*

—Gilles Deleuze, *Différence et répétition*

Klee at Carthage

> *Color possesses me.*
> *I don't have to pursue it.*
> —Paul Klee, *Notebooks*

That April in the sea-lit town, under fractal skies,
awakened to the sparkling syntax of the waves,

he followed shadow down the narrow alleyways
and climbed through olive-shouldered hillside groves

to seek out new complexions for the mind to wander in,
new towns where solids seemed to hang reflected

in the blistering air, as though he'd found—while wave
collapsed in particle and promptly fluidized as wave again—

Creation in an even older state than in that garden
where our naming claimed its firm possession of the light.

The Barbary sun enrobed him in its startling hues,
and wove an unnamed music in his sight, and all at once,

among these fragrant oleanders on the road, demanded
he apply to vividness the quanta of a finer scale, the haunting

microtones he'd heard in Persian song, the countless terms
for sand among the Bedouin, for ice among the Inuit.

Celestial Motion

on Five Cornell Assemblages in a Corner of the Museum

Each cell quavers softly on its quiet wall,
its atmosphere left open on one side. Yet,
blanketed in gases of its own, each one sits
outside this world, beside adjacent worlds
a world apart.

And while indecently exposed
to every peeping passerby, each one seems
a wholly independent universe alongside
other universes tightly cloisonnéd, each miracle
the monad of itself, each one an echo chamber
self-contained within this row of alien moons
and luminosities arrayed like shining bell-jars
in a lacquered cabinet of cosmic curiosities.

Regard how their unearthly atmospheres
appear to beckon entry from a distant light within,
but should you step too close to such precision,
such precise oblivion as this, its aloof,
indifferent, disdainful citizens
won't deign to let you in.

Verisimilitude

Funny how you just might think
you know what they are saying
in the intervals between the brush-
strokes and the obbligatos, to them-
selves, to one another, to the dead.

At certain times you think you're
onto what abstraction means, which goes
for content too, the way that all art's
referential, all art rooted in the world,
always carried by the breath, yet never
anything but abstract, abstracted
from the dubious evidence of sight
and sound, distracted by emotion.

And as you listen, you can think
you see, and watching, think you hear,
what's really going on out there, out
among the tangled concepts that give rise
to rhythm, melody, rare illumination,
out beyond the universe of explication,
out there in the distant world we live in,
way out west of the one we think in.

And funny how it is that some folks,
so comically inept at lying, cannot fail
to speak the truth in all the strange
unearthly sounds and images
and shapes they make.

And how sometimes in the presence
of a Turner, say, a Rothko, Bartok, Monk,
you really want to tell them,
Boy, you sure did get that right.
And ain't it just the way, though?
Goddamn. Ain't that
just the way?

Of Time and Weather

> *Time and space are modalities with which*
> *we think, not conditions in which we live.*
>   —Albert Einstein

Whatever did we know before we learned it?
What on earth did we possess before we found it?
Why did the flagrant world flash forth at all,
like lightning from a cloudless sky, and why
this rumbling noise of life, these fleeting cameos
that fasten to our intellect's discrete, caressing eye?

The world we seem to safely occupy,
this consoling hologram of depth and shadow,
this endless winding road we seem to travel,
is our planar, n-dimensioned atmosphere's
oblique projection of itself as something thought,
as distance, as the wandering course of time.

But what imaginings arise in these reflections,
these bright recursions in the mind! the way
the world avails itself of consciousness to find
in each examined dewdrop other worlds arrayed
within the smallest things, stranger worlds and larger far
than these in which they seem contained, where each

thing harbors what is vaster than itself, and teems
transfinite with the unchecked energies of life, with
unborn stuff of which the animate is made, that animates
what's never been alive, yet sets it whirling round
its dispossession, ever emptying, ever replicating
what's forever lost and time cannot contain.

Scissiparity

> ... *but realized to my dismay that the intruder was nothing other than my own reflection in the mirror of the open door. I still remember that I thoroughly disliked his appearance.*
> —Sigmund Freud, *Das Unheimliche*

You cannot see them both at once,
those two reflections in the glass:
the one that stands before you now,
what caught your interest as you passed.

This newly freshened image of yourself at rest,
composed, adjusted to your scrutinizing view,
such soothing restorations can't be reconciled
with the phantom of that grim preconscious you,

with the baseless malice of that perfect stranger,
a Doppelganger mirrored on that storefront space,
adrift among the pale reflections rushing past,
who only for an instant showed his face,

and for just one briefest moment held your rapt
attention fast as it aimed its hostile, predatory glare
directly at your fear, while mockery flickered
in its savage, cruel, unblinking stare.

Try as you might, you cannot hold these images
together or apart; the culprit here is time. What's past
has left you helpless in its grasp, upon a darkened
stage, among the empty streets of unrequited crime.

These multiples of one who stands before his
reconstructed self, each hazy mannequin you flee,
this solid, reassuring image in the glass, articulate
what's alien in you, and that which stirs in me.

This Excess Our Sentience

What is this bluster in our weather
that accumulates as thought? why these
bucking headwinds in the languid mind?

And why exactly does the alien thing appear
upon the vague horizons of attention?
Who is it ferrets through our waking sleep?

What is it out there always manages
to come unwrapped and fly apart?
What anxious energy inheres in things?

What is it in the modest distance
of the dormant other thing that seems
to animate the barricaded silences in you?

and summoning this lonely plenitude you are,
cannot ever seem to simply leave you be,
apart, aloft, adrift in mournful isolation?

Perhaps recumbent in the perfect stillness
we expect within ourselves, securely wrapped
inside each one who feels and thinks and speaks,

lies one who somehow isn't really you at all,
and from its unprotected quietude cannot otherwise
than rise, respond and interrupt your peace.

It seems sometimes as if your tidy separation
from the world out there'd been left to lie undone,
unfinished, inconvenienced at the very least,

by a separation so intense it's left a surplus
in its wake, some vital organ dangling out, some feral
stuff within, to leave you in this sorry state

where everything you see addresses you
in the senseless stammers of desire, the ever-present
voice of absence, some wholeness that you lack,

the yearnings of your porous skin, the qualms
of sentient flesh, the way mind's inconvenient
images arise at the distant end of black.

Among the Obstinate Nostalgias

The source of this insistence is no faculty,
no sly capacity of ours to recollect. This fretting
marks the feeble presence of the smallest things
that survive our feeble talent for forgetting.

They make of you a helplessly anachronistic thing,
these yearnings, each more ancient than the last,
and awakening, awaken you with sudden urgency,
en route to urgent assignations long since past.

You can't help notice how the steady spider-ants
of time have deftly stitched their patterns in the rain.
They've tightly woven shut the searching eye
and anxious ear, yet burrow in the buzzing brain

to haunt the outer boroughs of your thought,
provoke the furious peregrinations of your pen.

Emblems of Alterity

What cannot stand erect among the present things,
and can't be said to speak or seen to disappear,
what never hides or shows itself, or dwells
within the superfluities of atmosphere,

is nonetheless a supplication on the way to you,
the way desire insists in what you see and hear,
the way familiar strangers will defile your dreams
with unfamiliar dialects that linger in your ear

to prompt the concrete thought, arouse the abstract
skin, provoke the mute infuriations of your sleep
with insubstantial evidence of all you've lost
or sought to lose, and all you'd hoped to keep.

In Finitude

> *Man is in love and loves what vanishes,*
> *What more is there to say?*
> —WB Yeats, *Nineteen Hundred and Nineteen*

Morning hauls the dreamer
from her restless bed, reassembles
from the fragments of her sleep
the cowl of solitude
that daylight dwells in
and reconstitutes this thing
we think of as our peerless self,
the singularity that crouches
in its one specific skin
to view the world from deep
within a barricaded, finite space.

But time and circumstance
conspire against this privacy
we seek, this isolation we deplore,
to find this flesh of ours composed
of nocturnes left exposed
to blind indifference and distraction,
by prospects likely never known,
the fleeting vulpine contour
of a shadow in the juniper,
an ancient roar of armies in the dark,
the anxious swish of poplars
in the streambed or the stillness
of a marshland ibis
in the dreamscape
of an unfamiliar dusk.

She who rises from the night
remains by day a creature
of the night, a cryptic congeries,
when all is said and done,
of random, barely noticed things,
a motley stitched from all
that got away, each thing
that never really was,
of all the jumbled detritus
that constitutes this rattle-bag
of dreaming and oblivion we are,
of partial things and things forgotten,
things misplaced, discarded or unnoticed,
the precisely factored product
of all we've lost, ignored,
abandoned: of all we cannot
manage to possess.

It's from the unobtainable,
it seems, from the irrecoverable,
that we derive uniqueness.
It's this one specific constellation
of losses tells us who we are,
that fabricates each subject,
every someone subject to the world,
that builds the glorious, deviant self
and excavates each sentient body's
clamorous, formless, depthless,
unfathomable interior.

And I say more. That the limit-
less perishability of all the things
of this world, their clearly labeled
shelf-life, is precisely our affiliation
with the infinite, with what beckons
and persists but cannot be obtained,
the relentless rapport of our intensely finite,
intensely subject selfhood with all
that lies beyond its grasp, the precious
substance of life's incessant,
uneasy, fruitless dialog
with eternity.

Street People

Des rides énormes labouraient son front.
—Gustave Flaubert, *La légende de Saint Julien l'Hospitalier*

He importunes you gently
in the narrow side-street, politely,
almost timidly, mumbling a supplication
you don't quite catch, extending
a grey-black, fingerless glove
from under a greasy greatcoat
hanging loose from tall shoulders
on windy afternoons in spring—
his attire in all weathers—to expose
the briefest flash of elaborate vest,
a sublimated brocade of some sort,
gone dark with time and grime,
over still further layers
of sooty coverings: a collarless shirt,
a crew-necked undergarment,
an elaborately knotted scarf, perhaps,
and leather hat, and did we see it right
in the shady passageway that day?
silver buttons were they,
winking from the desolations
of that scurvy, tattered vest of his?

I'm not sure how we could
have taken this all in,
that morning in the narrow lane,
our eyes cast fixedly down,
as though deep in revery,
as though the pavement
harbored latent treacheries,
and knitted our brows
in exaggerated concentration
as he hove into sight
a half-block ahead, like a ghostly ship
or piratical corsair sailing
grandly toward us.

We nattered on intently,
determined to evade the awkwardness
of eye-contact, and remained
in mute denial
for a full two seconds after
barely registering the gentle,
courtly speech that issued
from his direction, from somewhere
troublingly near, from a source
that seemed too close for comfort,
as we breezed past that voice
in our fabricated haste.

But sheepishly we stopped
an instant later, and swung round,
and as we fumbled guilt-stricken
through our pockets
for some loose change
or small bills, and as he swirled
and hugely hurtled past, repeated
what we'd struggled to ignore:
"Back there, gentlemen,
you dropped your package."

***

I encountered him again last week,
in that same neighborhood,
different street, and stopped to watch
from a shady doorway as he detached
from a sidewalk congregation
of fellow panhandlers to approach,
palms up, an elderly couple,
all the while maintaining
a discrete distance
(so as not to alarm?)
and I imagined the melody
his voice must be making then,
from my cool, dispassionate distance,
that voice I'd barely heard that day,
but which lingered in my ear, gentle,
courteous, unashamed,
and tried to ambush from afar
a glimpse of his expression
as the startled vacationers bustled past him,

and searching for some small sign
of mockery in that eye, or contempt
or bitterness, snatched only
the ebony glint of a cheekbone
as his indifferent burning gaze, the gaze
I'd so often feared to engage,
panned right past me.

And it struck me then
that while this stranger had become
an outsized factor in my life,
I myself had no earthly role in his,
that all we had in common, the two of us,
all we shared, all that connected us,
was the unavoidable fact
of our irreconcilable differences,
the shadow of an unfathomable disparity,
and that he, approaching me
in another system than the happenstance
of our coincidence in time and space,
like the intimate, disquieting angels
that visit us in sleep,
would never, could never,
acknowledge my presence.

***

Jacob, it is told,
wrested from his angel a blessing,
after his night-long combat.
That blessing that he sought, I imagine,
was just perhaps some hint
of simple recognition, some evidence
of his existence, his inclusion in that angel's
world, in his impersonal laser-gaze. And I
deeply doubt his biblical victory,
but not at all the drama of the struggle,
for such victory would require
a suspension of the laws of nature,
a miraculous hiatus
in the physics of desire.

And so I tried to imagine
my own formidable,
darkly towering angel's face
close up, whose fearful sight
I'd once so anxiously avoided,
and imagined the sound of such words
as he refused us then, a quavering
noise of need, and I was unable to do so,
and failing that, I turned and left,
and returning to my noisy day,
I found this brush with chance had left
my emptied selfhood compromised,
eclipsed, and in the end,
I must gratefully admit,
though unaccountably nourished,
irretrievably bereft.

The Gaze of Another

Night Thoughts on Street People

*Le visage du prochain . . . échappe à la
représentation. Il est la défection même
de la phénoménalité.*
—Emmanuel Levinas

The gaze of another
occludes the other's face,
the otherness alive in every face,
the nonspecific countenance
an appearance for which
I'm never quite prepared,
from whose direction
the unmitigated gaze
strikes like lightning
on a cloudless day in Spring,
without warning.

That gaze of his is not
another object of my sight,
lying out at the horizon
of my observation, not man
or mountain or tree or lighthouse,
nothing my sharpest discernment
may come to rest upon,
not available to me
as are those images
and projections,
however penetrating,
however haunting,
that I may hold at arm's length
in an album of photographs,

or behold on a gallery wall,
or calmly contemplate
from my secure position
in the world, surveilled
from the comfort of my loge
in a darkened theater.

The gaze of another,
in its startling carnality,
the gaze that issues
from the Other,
from a place I assume
the other creature to occupy,
is an unforeseen calamity,
a lethal, alternating current,
beckoning but repellent,
pleading and accusing,
a devouring event horizon
into which I tumble,
stripped of every armor,
disarmed of any shelter,
without a plausible alibi,
without proof of identity,
but which identifies
and specifies me alone
as the naked fact
of this precipitating self,
this plummeting that's me,
this creature tumbling
newborn into the mute,
pleading indigence
of a gaze I am
in no position to return.

It is this inadequacy,
this withering calamity,
not thought, I think,
that is the real *cogito* of our being
in this world, proof positive
of the wobbly state of dispossession
we call existence, and the foundation
of all our febrile industry,
the instigation of all
our eager inquiry.

But life itself, it seems,
the effortlessness
of our abiding, pure and simple,
offers countless resources, presents
a million stratagems
for indifference, tactics
to which we all must resort.

For we "habituate ourselves,"
as Proust would say, or better yet
this life habituates us,
familiarizes the face of the neighbor,
the stranger, the face of the companion,
of the enemy, of each circumstantial
place that we manage to occupy
and furnish with the familiar.

We have no choice in the matter,
since this process of habituation
just happens to us, happens in the world
of the possible, constructs a world of possibility,
but takes place as an involuntary product
of the passage of Time,
where effectiveness and possibility
might easily overpower the gaze,
and thereby make room for us,
clear a space for intention, and give us time
for anticipation, reflection, preemption.

And, for a time, such habituation
will grant us the capacity
to transact our business, the largesse
with which to contemplate our lot,
and from the imperial indifference
of our boundless freedom, permit
the exercise of choice and decision,
establish a stable-seeming place from which
we might observe the world unseen,
at liberty to volunteer affection
or contempt, practice charity
or visit violence, as we see fit,
upon the faceless,
defenseless neighbor.

But always in that private, shaded
solitary space of sequestration,
where cool decision dwells,
we encounter such a solitude
as will not leave us simply be,
where dwells another logic
of the self, another time,
where oh so softly speaks
the unheard otherness of things,
where meaning issues darkly
from the featureless gaze of another,
where intimations couched
in unfamiliar rhythms indistinctly speak
in words I cannot fathom.

Incompletion Ode

> *... deformed, unfinished, sent before my time*
> *into this breathing world scarce half made up ...*
> —William Shakespeare, *Richard III*

We can't be whole and somehow also be.
In wholeness lies our dream of death,
our dreams of dreamless sleep, self's silent
circle left alone to dream itself in blessed exile

from the instigating otherness in things.
It is the phantom image of our frantic flight
from all the wondrous woundedness we bear,
the susceptivities of questing flesh

that some call spirit, some call mind,
this savage incompletion that we are, exposed
to every transient thought and hope and fear,
to life's incessant violation of the house

that seems to stir the air somewhere outside
the self, but interrupts this solitude, this desperate
dream of wholeness, with an imprecise disquiet
at the bone, a distant rummaging within.

III

*A tree-
high thought
clasps the soundlight: there are
still songs to sing beyond
mankind.*

—Paul Celan, *Fadensonnen*

. . . is the carbon molecule lined with thought?

—Saul Bellow, *Herzog*

Visitations of Spring

April howls along the eaves.
Winter's silver bird has flown.

Winter's dire dove has fled
before the mad rejoicings.

The annotations of our minor key,
these iron mountains, rise

like thrusting spires of Lupin,
Foxglove, grasping Jessamine,

to muscle through the noisy night,
through darkest dreams of Hellebore,

this world arrayed in magnitudes,
spring's hawkmoth-haunted hour.

Volunteers

Our late arrival
        Mexican Hat
bejewels the orchard floor
        patchwork product
of morning's desultory
        here and there

of all its long-agos
        and seasons-since
the random bijouterie
        of countless
aimless self-seedings
        eager volunteer

who surfaces like thought
        quickens to the voice
of seasons always gone
        just as reason rallies
summoned into being
        by the frantic flesh

reporting for duty
        at best an instant late
the intempestive
        hapless product
of mind's nostalgia
        for the fugitive signals

skins receive the way
        all conscious things
all sentient life all bright
        excrescences of time
all incarnations
        of our presence here

occur only after the fact
        only after experience
to occupy the twilight
        of an *arrière-pensée*
since all thoughts are nought
        but second thoughts after all.

Eos

for Lauralyn Eschner

Mornings in the orchard, early May,
the stiffened hosepipes burp and spit.
By noon the light may threaten June,
but May's a paper tiger here.

The silence of these naked limbs
reflects our springtime's dithering sky,
but any day I'll find their languid possum sleep
adorned with emerald and pearls of early pink
that lead us on to budbreak, leaf-break,
half-inch green, into the concupiscent air,
the rude processions of awakening.

There's a novel softness in the breeze today,
the sap is rising; a shrill uncivil singing fills the ear.

While every weather sees this orchard
and its keeper getting on in years,
we've learned we cannot overestimate
the way, from desiccated sticks,
new signs of life, new melodies, arise
to meet the swirling season, the way
new wine arrives, always and again,
in the fullness of relentless time, to fill
these thirsty skins of ours, to slake
this mortal flesh as if in answer
to the yearnings of this gathering,
this scarified, this always
resurrected skin.

Flyfishing

Membrane rises   veined with liquid   lifted by the sun
by sublimations risen   from the incoherent   surface
of the deep   by the unremitting   sculpting dew
that canyons   mountains   in its wandering descent
imparting nutriment   endowing verdure   making new.

Thus something   draws us   from the noisy ground
onto the quiet spit   where anglers   cast their filament
to sparkle   in the rippling air   above the prolix stream
across the urgent   incoherent discourse   of the element.

The poet too   is like an angler   at the extremity
of sense   dumbstruck on the tangled   bank of meaning
pursuing every   savage iridescence   each furtive shadow
in the rill   each subaquatic carol   drawn from dreaming.

As Gravity Builds Bone

It's gravity's tenacious grasp
resists the fiber's braided rise
to prompt the angering bone.

It's daylight beckons into being
each tender gathering leaf
and glazes every searching eye,

while dark aromas excavate
the eager nostril in reply
to what's no longer there,

and feathered cochlea coil to fix
incarnate every feral tremor
stirring in the vacant air.

Just so, each body that we are
is sculpted of the world entire
as scar, investiture or mute response

to all that lies outside of us, a world
outside the will, before the self,
each sinew of our provenance.

Jellyman

Dispatch from the Center of the Known Universe

> *I seem to have been given the freedom*
> *of this place what am I then?*
> Ted Hughes, *Woodwo*

It's a question
of where it is this here might be
of why our languid viscid drift slither ooze
across its landscape where we bathe sustained
arrested shaped encumbered from all sides this tender
ushering unsheltering membrane's slave to every tiny gradient
itch each transient flux the endless fluency of our surroundings
the monotonies the surfaces and ondulations of these lachrymal
galvanic seas where held apart within a sentience stationed far too
close to things exposed to all the noiseless nearness here alert alive
awake in search of any heat of any likely edge in reach hemmed in
by every pulse and vagary those barely theres that radiate transect that violate this frail frontier which shouldn't really be
we oddly feel whatever's there or barely gone and
dream what's only not and stranger still the
inconvenient fact of all this endless
swaying space outside our fluid
saline amniotic
thought

Physics 101

> *It rises from the depths and ascends into*
> *the sky, its voice filling the spring winds*
> *that scatter autumn leaves.*
> —David Hinton, *The Four Chinese Classics*

When the distant mountain rumbles,
dragon is that distance.

When dragon coils in coiling air,
this turbulence is dragon.

As dragon spirals, coil on coil,
these spirals are the circling days

that cycle in the circling blood,
and churn like starlings overhead.

* * *

Dragon breathes water, fire, flesh
and stone. In and out. In and out.

When dragon shakes his mighty head
and laughs, this laughter is our grief and joy.

Dragon dances, capers, makes its way
so slowly you won't notice, yet

her velocity can take your breath away,
this swiftness you and dragon share.

You cannot yield to dragon, can't resist.
So sorry; there's no higher power there.

* * *

Dragon isn't something hidden everywhere,
or something nowhere to be found,

since dragon never will appear at all,
except in all that sightless folks imagine

drifting on the scaly underside of cloud,
in the courtly pomp of seasons,

across the stately nighttime sky,
above the veiled saltpeter moon,

in every feral dream's meanderings,
in thunder's flashing light, the creeping tide,

the scratching noise of nineteen sunsets,
each slashing pen and whispering brush,

the slither of a woven belt through belt-loops,
a roaring Norton's throaty whine.

* * *

In dragon is the gaiety of atmosphere,
the madness in our sky,

the aimless paths we wander, day by day,
the twisting galleries of our desire,

the emptiness of troubled seas,
time's looping arabesques arrayed

beneath her jeweled lid, her coppery flanks,
the flicker of her half-remembered eye.

* * *

When springtime's swollen rivers roar,
this turmoil is the thrashing tail of dragon.

When someone watches from the mirror,
this stranger is the utter foreignness of dragon.

When stillness settles in the evening air,
such reticence is the purling voice of dragon.

Absent at the Dawn of Creation

*The most incomprehensible thing about
the world is that it is comprehensible.*
        —Albert Einstein

Morning's dawn exploded from the ridge
with a shout today, setting all the dripping leaves
and sailing clouds ablaze, declaring itself arisen
with the brio of heralding brass in the *Resurrexit*
of the B minor Mass. But this celestial fanfare
arose without a sound—almost.

Somewhere in the distance, a magpie scolded.
Everywhere, the softly dripping aftermath
of an early morning downpour. Wandering
overhead, dark cumuli abruptly cancelled
the patinating light. One moment to the next,
these oscillations stripped the glitter
from the leaves, and just as soon,
they'd incandesce as if the morning's brash
arrival seemed to need a period of settling-in,
required a decent interval of temporizing pulses
to relax the grip of night.

Otherwise, the stillness in the air was absolute.
So absolute, you'd swear that it had made
a presence in your ear, a thing like sound,
a noiseless rush, a deafening hush whose
pressure seemed to hold the leaf, the breath,
the morning light and morning dusk,
and all the trembling planets, in suspense.

And what exactly was your place, your role
in all of this? you remember thinking then.
What room was left there in that silent world
for the busy whirring of your silent thought?
You, who could not manage to remain
outside it all, and could not somehow enter in?
What vantage point was granted you, granted
to your searching ear and penetrating eye?
What special privileged place from which
to contemplate in calm repose the miracle
of dawn's prodigious sky?

None of these, I think, no place at all. It is
as if we stand aside and watch, it seems to me,
as if all thought takes place at the farthest margins
of the real, as if the seeing eye, the listening ear
and thinking brain—creations, incarnations,
of the vibrant world around us, its ownself formed
of pure vibration and unbridgeable distances,
extruded from reality like light, like matter—
may only occupy that wild, remote, eccentric place
assigned us by the world entire, to accept the fate
that's ours alone, and with this solitary flesh,
this bleak haphazard thought, this croaking voice
and jangling lyre, give praise, as Rilke says,
give praise for every briefest gift, each bright
disastrous dawn, each god-forsaken squall,
all sudden onslaughts of a brazen sunlight blazing
on the blistered plaster of your garden wall.

Georgics in a Plague Year

Down in the busy silence, the humic dark
that dreams beneath the parching surface
of this orchard, fungal fingers in their trillions reach
in all directions through the teeming duff,
thrusting obligatory charity into the copious unseen,
insinuating their air-gathered, nitrous nurture
ever outward through the verging rootzones
of this soil's woody progeny, up into the canopy
under which we wander out each morning, drawn
through the foliar shadowland of this soil's stately,
ecstatic upwellings, into the verdure that extracts
from us an impromptu litany of naming as we pass:
*Esopus Spitzenburg, Calville Blanc d'Hiver, Brown Snout,
Cox's Orange Pippen, Tompkins County King.*

Elsewhere on the fringes of these orchestrated plantings,
deep in the quiet of a juniper's shade, elsewhere
in this dimensionless, möbial surface of gas, rock,
peat and sentient tissue that is nature's space,
our ubiquitous prodigal and paragliding pollinator,
dread *Ichneumon,* Burrowing Wasp, mantles
over her ill-starred cicada, posterity's preferential,
iridescent nursery, and deftly insinuates between
its lustrous, chitinous plates the paralyzing ovipositor,
enacts her terminal, murderous, immemorial maternity,
and inflicts at her own expense the heartless immolation
life requires, delivering her progeny to incubate, emerge,
and devour the living entrails of the hapless host
in the grip of an exigent future, a recurrence,
she herself will never see.

Thus, the uncompromising ethic of this world,
the nature of our Nature, is spoken everywhere
in this garden, this *pardes,* this unremitting holocaust
of transpiration and expiration, this carnival
of fecundity, theater of cruelty and boundless goodness
and nourishing waste, heedless of our human sentiment,
to expose the life of all the living as here and always
the martyrdom of another, ever an expense
of the predecessor, everywhere the sacrificial gift
of the merciless, magnanimous, unwitting neighbor.

And if truth indeed be beauty, girl, whose vivid
spectacle confounds us in this place, the truth
of this and all the wide world's endless beauty,
ah my Juliana, is never ever easy.

Pastoral

The canyon walls above our orchard
magnify the rock squirrel's sharp report,
the news that death's been spotted skulking
somewhere in the neighborhood, caparisoned
as bullsnake, Harris Hawk, or ghostly coyote.

Our dogs are masters of this semeiotics
of the scolding magpie or apoplectic jay,
and hope eternally to ambush unawares
the predator himself, beguiled, enthralled,
distracted by the presence of his prey.

While these diligent dogs' scant record
of performance, I'll admit, is anything
but stellar, and their success rate hovers
right at zero, I, who occupy the role of hero,
have learned from them how meanings seem

to summon us obliquely in an unfamiliar voice
from the faint collaterals of our rapt attention,
from a speaking spoken elsewhere than the locus
of our fascination, as a whispered chorus, antiphon
or admonition we're only all too happy to ignore.

The Dragons of Paradise

But never met this fellow / Attended or alone
Without a tighter breathing / And zero at the bone—
                      —Emily Dickinson

And suddenly the upright world went tilt,
while daylight's dubious blue blazed
oddly at her left. Abruptly, she awoke
to find her level world's horizon angled
strangely upward through the trees.
In the eerie clarity of her dislocation,
she realized that everything had changed.

She lay quiet as a corpse, observing
in fascination the parade of gargantuan ants
that scrambled over her arm. Resurfacing
bit by bit into the familiar grid of time
and swirling space, some modicum of calm
returned her to herself, to the absurdity
of her situation, and taking stock, she somehow
found herself herself again, herself as someone else,
an avatar of self, diminished, disarranged,
abruptly reduced to a crumpled heap
of vivid housedress draped
across the graveled walk.

She must have hit her head.
She felt the gritty scratch of pathway
on her cheek, and noticed all at once,
rising into her ribcage, the stabbing ache
of a shattered thigh absurdly folded
underneath her weight. Motionless,
paralyzed with pain and dread,
she darkly knew its cause, and knew
there was no chance of help in easy earshot,
way out here at her little pond, at the far end
of the garden, out beside the canyon rim.

The caustic ache washed over her
in waves. Through the peculiar logic
of her delirium, she seemed to hover
somewhere outside the scene to contemplate
her world engulfed in roaring flame,
consumed in dragon's breath.
Somewhere in the distance,
monsoon thunderheads lined up
out behind the mountains.

**

There's an ozone sweetness in the air today,
as Father Jerry from his shaded bench
inhales the pungent emanations of soft viridian
and burnt sienna rising from the canyon,
and puzzles at those peculiar little structures
that ring the pond like tiny tumbledown bathhouses,
barely upright, choked, after the passing
of the years, with clumps of Joe Pie Weed
and Prickly Pear, and recollects her patient
explanation of their peculiar mission.

*I knocked them all together out of scrap-wood
in the shed*, she'd said, *The rattlers smell
our water here, and seem attracted to this place,
but this pond in daylight heat is so exposed,
they seemed to need some sanctuary space,
some little ashrams where, it seemed to me,
in summer they'd find shelter from this blasted sun.*

Back then, she'd tease him mercilessly. *O thou
wise apostate, long-lapsed postulate, just tell me straight,*
she'd say, *are we just bodies here, or are we air?
Tell me now, just where does your infernal "spirit" lie?
down here in time? or in some vaporous shadow realm,
in hopes of its eventual reward, awaiting the arrival
of a hard-earned, purpose-built eternity?*

Exasperated by the hem and haw of his replies,
she'd snort her genial disapproval, and turn
abruptly to her pruning.

***

He wonders now, on this same little bench
beside the pond by which she'd spent
her lonely final hours, what stammering response
he might have conjured all those years ago,
in her grouchy company out by the canyon rim,
while the silent seed malignly ripened in her thigh.

And today, as his dozing contemplations
drift and ruminate upon the shrewd design
and forlorn spectacle of those spavined little shelters,
there occurs to him an altogether different way
of understanding, a new vernacular he'd often struggled
to extrude from thought, an unrehearsed response
to her persistent interrogations that seemed,
after long gestation, to tumble headlong,
without effort, without resistance, albeit now
a decade late, into the indifferent evening air.

*I think this thing we call the soul must not
be anything we have,* he murmurs in the fading light,
*but an impropriety that overturns the self,
insinuations of that thing we are that isn't ever ours
at all, perhaps, no object or possession of our own,
like an earlobe or a pancreas, but the abstract logic
of our giving and our loss, the very dispossession
that defines this way we seem to be, this thing
we are but cannot ever own.*

It's just perhaps the gauzy name we use
for that unwitting madness in ourselves
that cannot otherwise than muster a response
to the untimely, the unsettling, the unfamiliar,
that reacts instinctively with violence or fear
to the inauspicious alien that loiters in its alien skin,
but just might somehow leave us space
to welcome what's most foreign to our self,
accommodate the noontime's startling hiss of menace,
our unremitting zero at the bone, that noiseless
voice from somewhere in the flesh,
that always leaves the self behind
and leaves behind itself the priceless speckled gift
of all we've ever lost and loved, and all
that what's called living gives away.

***

Somewhere to the east, monsoon thunder
rumbled in the summer sky. She was in and out.
Awakened briefly by a few fat raindrops
on her cheek, she saw, or seemed to see,
some feet away, the slack procession
of a noiseless, coiling cloisonné,
an exquisite tracery of bright enamels,
something fluid, molten, gliding
through the rocks beside the pond,
bound for shelter, solicited by shadow
into the warping pressboard refuge
of her little canopies.

The Sisyphus of Demolition

Systematically, she unbuilds the pile
of fruitwood I'd artfully stacked here
last autumn, apple boughs and pear,
our fragrant fuel so neatly cantilevered,
to dry beside the fire-pit, awaiting
the hungry tongues of flame, the pallid Wagyu
tomahawk or lamb-leg, an evening
of windless weather made for roasted chiles,
for the chef's privilege of numerous tequilas,
for a celebration of twenty-odd votive candles
line-dancing at twilight down the center
of the old pine table by the greenhouse.

Of course, I know what she's after,
my dog Rose. She seeks a favorite saurian
snack of whiptail, skink or collared lizard
that she's detected skittering
through the myriad passageways
of this airy condominium, all the way
from her napping spot in the Dharma Garden.
Up and dashing to the site, homing in
on the telltale rustle, she peers down upon
the little woodpile, neck arched, ears forward,
happy horsewhip tail waving, her athletic frame
poised for a sudden pounce,
but she doesn't. Instead,

she begins to paw at the little log-splits,
not vigorously, but surgically, in exploratory mode,
with her intuitive grasp of statics, first
from one side of the stack, then from another,
and finding the single-point failure options
of this little ziggurat, brings it neatly down to grade,
where she can sort the rubble, spread it out,
wonder where the lizards went, and watch as I,
uttering little grunts of exasperation,
gather in the scattered members
of my clever structure, restore some
feeble verticality and walk away, peevishly
proposing she fill her cakehole elsewhere.

I am pretty certain Rose regards me
as at minimum some exotic brand
of intelligent life-form. I think I see it
in those looks she gives me, don't you?
their blend of skepticism and adoration,
bemusement, sympathy and incredulity.
So I imagine she wonders, at times
like this, what I must be up to, reassembling
a perfectly dismantled woodpile,
apparently indifferent to the tantalizing prospect
of some residual, errant, panicked prey,
the toothsome *cnemidophor*
or savory *crotaphyte*.

But at least our complementary roles in life
are clear and understood: she forever
seeking useful forage, I forever
blithely challenging gravity.

IV

This infinite improbability from which I've sprung lies beneath me like a void . . . the endless, dolorous improbability of this irreplaceable being that I am.

—Georges Bataille, *L'expérience intérieure*

Sgraffito

to a Snapshot's Ancient Child

Trusting the man behind the camera,
you commit your wide, brown, lonely gaze,
the artless translucence of your gamin skin,
the delicacy of your full-lipped, hesitant,
tolerating smile and narrow, fragile shoulders
unreservedly to that prurient lens and to the years,
as you tumble headlong, unwary, into the silent
ravages of the unforeseen, the subtle coruscations
of the unimaginable, the unhurried work of time.

You and I live without rapport, you who
perch politely heedless in your Tokyo kitchen,
painstakingly posed by the shutterbug stepfather,
blithely facing the unknown (For what
are the tadpole's thoughts of the frog's life
it has in store?), while I sit here, at the far side
of your existence, on a high-desert mountainside,
prospecting this ancient photo's halftones
for substantiations of the promising ore-body,
the telling evidence of raw material, any clues
that might reveal the rough stuff lives are made of.

You and I live without rapport, old child,
for your sweet vacuity projects contented plenitude,
a self-sufficiency obviating mystery, a tacit acceptance
of the happenstance that surrounds you, while I,
your beholder, retrospective, scarified by experience,
incised by the excavating passage of the years,
can only scrutinize this fragile composition of light
and shadow, as if its two scant dimensions
just might harbor some profound thing, some
cavernous lagoon of truth, blue-black with meaning.

The bright-eyed composure of this wary child
reveals the work of time as unrelenting subtraction,
construes the world as a quiet passage of ablations
and erosions, chiselings that leave behind a filigree
of lacework, serrations and receding planes, complex
as the canyoned gypsum crystals we call desert rose,
each excavated, knife-edged self, contrived by chance,
by heredity's caprice: a scouring of the elements, created
not of whole cloth, but by the obstinate rasp of time.

The Bonds of Separation

> *I am sitting here now with my father's eyes*
> —Yehuda Amichai

I think sometimes I catch you
watching warily from your picture-frame
above the garden books, Max Brumer!
me in my sloppy cotton shirt
and cargo shorts, you in natty top-hat,
white tie and tails. In the 1900 Federal Census,
you listed "Pants" as your profession.

I imagine you two whispering, teeth clenched,
my *gute babe* Rosa, smiling in her black lace gown,
benignly corsaged beside you—*Just who is
this little unkempt goy who set us here?*
you're asking, *those two big dogs asleep
beside him, declaiming into the book-lined room
his flattened, growling vowels, this inelegant
vernacular of his? And why does he insert
his brash exotic speech into this long-dead
mouth of mine?*

So what is it you want already? I imagine
Rosie replying. *You and I appear to be guests
here in this pretty little frame. Besides,
do you notice how intently he stares at us?
Brazen, almost rudely, as if we were guilty
of some crime in that mysterious future of his, guilty
of concealing evidence perhaps?
But something in this fellow reminds me, dear,
of your own grandfather, Rabbi Szmuil
of blessed memory, always buried
in his Talmud, and not unlike this boy,
always muttering to himself a little song.*

Or so I imagine you conversing there,
some short weeks after disembarking the *Palatia*
from Bremen, in that little studio on Delancey,
in all your finery. And I do perhaps stare
too intently at this sepiaed image, at the shadow
of lips and lids and knuckles at rest, and do not
find myself there. Yet photographs, I reckon,
only speak to us in riddles, cannot ever
show the hurried step, the subtle flicker
of living's crooked smile.

Great Grandfather, in the 1900 Census
you listed "Pants" as your profession.
And just today, we found our 2020 Census Bureau
Questionnaire in a plastic bag, down by the road,
hanging on the padlocked orchard gate.
Perhaps I'll grab a pen and open up
its envelope this afternoon. But how exactly,
I've already begun to wonder, shall I list there
my occupation?

Genealogies

We creatures of chance, children
of a stunning improbability,
are all infinitely more likely
never to have been. This is the math
of our uniqueness, the callous calculus
of our identity. Every last child
of parentage, each bright consequence
of statistical near-impossibility
and immemorial encounters stands
in the stream of which he's made,
and is himself this turgid stream,
this alluvial convergence, this brief
ingathering of countless teeming
tributaries of life.

My own mighty confluence
of compound coincidence
begins and ends right here,
plunges abruptly into the void,
absurdly out of sight, to vaporize
in the round earth's roiling mantle
or dissipate across the braided networks
of some broad telluric plain,
into an everywhere as featureless
as Dante's third circle, trickling
into every nowhere-in-particular.

I whisper the *Shema*'s bright fragment
upon this happy, childless house
each time I enter, remembering to listen,
to confer this blessing upon all of you
who end here, upon all the studious rabbis,
their eternally accommodating rebbetzin,
the ancient dreams and terrors and aspirations,
the burly, pragmatic expressmen, fastidious
needlemen and cabbies and confidence-men

whose shtetl blood I carry everywhere
with me, like buckets from the well.

All these bold frontiersmen
once ferried the restless blood
across a perilous water, into the roiling
confluences of another world, debarking
onto Delancey Street or Second Avenue,
as if to graft their bone and sinew
onto our beloved Whitman's xenophilic
"wooded flesh" along with all the Norman,
Saxon and Scots-Irish donors
to this howling mongrel blood of mine,
those grim believers fastening like limpets
onto Narragansett's desperate shore,
pushing fretfully into the dread penumbra
of a dense Kentucky wood, busting
into Minnesota hardscrabble, bearing
in their stolid knees and knuckles
the trace of long-forgotten nobilities.

These all secure the murmured blessings
conferred upon these bright enameled *mezuzot*
in earnest lip-service, bestowed upon these venerable
lines of flesh, the Ezras, Leahs and Lizzies,
the Benjamins, Lionels, Gitels and Rebekkahs
that end precisely here, as with the endless
Solomons lined up all the way back,
back perhaps even to the temple, even
to the guttered enclosures built to mimic
the upwelling spring of our first garden,
whose waters once divided to create, as Islam's
prophet tells us, the earth's four great rivers,
bringing liquid life to every cornered surface
of the many-tissued, brightly hued,
and many-peopled world.

With me these ancient multitudes,
these children of the waters,
leave no blood behind, no flesh
of their flesh, but only this modest
scattering of words, and the lengthy litany,
the fast-retreating melody, of their names.

Instructions for the Memoirist

on J.J. Rousseau's Confessions

Go measure out three yards of cloth
(you'd better make it four),
of lightweight weave that seems to suit
the guises you once wore.

Be sure you've purchased all you need
to cover, neck to floor,
the body of life's evidence,
what critics have in store.

You'll need whatever's left, my friend,
to patch up what you trim,
the naked truth, the cruelest cuts,
the best-omitted whim.

And save your scraps to cleverly disguise
all errors and omissions,
as time subjects your honest views
to multiple editions.

I recommend you not indulge
your taste for verbal finery,
for gold brocade or damask trim,
or obvious chicanery,

Except perhaps some moiré silk,
some Shandong or some crepe,
to line the thing with slippery stuff,
in case you must escape.

And when you think that you are done,
approach your three-way mirror,
but notice, as you pull this garment on,
 your features disappear.

No perspicacities of tact and candor,
no deft embroideries of age and youth,
can put to rest the pen's meander,
the memory's subtle substitutes for truth.

Smashing Atoms with a Hammer

on Revisiting My Vesalius

I write of melancholy, by being busy to avoid melancholy
—Robert Burton, *The Anatomy of Melancholy*

Help me please make certain no one ever learns
I haven't the foggiest what boredom means.
Do not speak of it, if you would kindly please,
lest insistent ringing rouse the drowsing phone,
relentless rapping shake my dreaming door.

I've seen that look of horror at the cocktail hour
illuminate the vacant social smile and ragdoll eye,
and animate with dark distrust the haggard mien
of men who took me for a fellow traveler of theirs
along their weedy road, among the upright dead.

I never really learned the art of pregnant sighs,
the urbane world's world-weary melodies,
though I've known the grip of grief and paralyzing loss,
those passageways, airless as ever O'Neill walked
or Lowry, the many-branched arterials of sorrow.

But what to make of all this richly sinewed space,
the frolicsome perversity of every liquid, living thing,
the curious manners and mannerisms all around,
the other voices, other rooms, the sparkling ripeness
of the stars that energize this dusty, crawling world?

And what of thought, and what of dream (the earth's
ecstatic skin), this hunger hurtling forward into dark?
I never learned to jettison this bright blunt instrument,
the dawdling mind, its endless appetite, this ceaseless,
senseless hammering at heaven's adamantine door.

All Knowledge Is Carnal

And gather me / Into the artifice of eternity
    —WB Yeats, *Sailing to Byzantium*

I

That was the time of sounding brass,
where chime and ululation beckoned
from behind the cloistering garden walls
and drifted through the alleyways he'd climb
at Fez to flee the noisome reek of boiling
lamb and coriander. In that taciturn
and tender space, each speechless voice
implied seduction, while meaning always
stood aloof, a silent vestal in that firmament
of cryptic gesture and unsampled flesh.

II

Then other mountains, other skies,
and endless winding shores, as all
the years like mounted lancers calmly passed,
and road-dust settled on his anxious skin,
while dreams of always imminent departure,
of rusty packets bound for Tripoli, Aleppo, Crete
or Trebizond, of trackless sands and featureless
terrains, construed within his sedentary mind
a hypersphere of lust and paradox, a convoluted
phantasy of empty, vast, imagined distances.

III

And here and there a wave-slapped pier,
the winking dance of harbor-lights, the roar
of swaying pines, a bitter heaving tide,
the evening's slumbering hills and lambent skies,
the melancholy minarets of dawn. Yet somewhere
at the outskirts of a dream, he sensed time's
imprint on the murmuring skin and mumbling
intellect, recognized the rumor of its breath
in sleep, its passage through the tangled brain,
its voice among the tumbling cataracts of song.

IV

This frail serenity he'd finally come to wander in
sits brightly on the plain, a luminescent reverie
of Isfahan or bronze Khartoum, an angle of repose
that accumulated time and loss and longing built,
where the hard-earned laws of living calmed
the panic in his blood and made a modicum of room
in which his careful mind might dimly comprehend
the austere patterns of desire, embrace the distant
diapsons of cymbal drum and string, contrive to wake
the sweet, persistent, feral noise that meanings make.

Not the Landscape

> *Success is like some horrible disaster*
> *Worse than your house burning.*
> —Malcolm Lowry, *After the Publication of Under the Volcano*

This is not the landscape of your long-held dream,
the dream at last arrived, the dream that on arrival
disassembled all the yearning world that radiated
from the consolations of your bygone yearning self,
that by arriving turned you loose among the unfamiliar
contours of an unfamiliar space, and whose arrival
sent your trusty compass needle spinning in its case.

Good fortune's frayed the labyrinthine webwork
of life's departed circumstance and all the filaments
desire wove, the exquisite embroidery of need,
the steadfast gravitation that secured you to the ground.

The constant dream that shaped the needful world
in which you moved has come unglued. And here,
where what you wished has come to pass, you find
yourself another creature, creature of another mind
and alien race, the child of other yearnings, other loss,
bewildered by the landforms your desires left behind.

Anamneses

In the scant light of grief,
you cannot help but notice
how the bookshelves all turn grey,
the way each furtive spineless title
starts to rummage for its coat and keys,
now that all the band's packed up
and bound for home, and all that's left
of life's bright dancing song
is the desultory jarring clink
of dirty teacups in the sink.

Oddly, you persist in seeing
grief as that which lies ahead,
and in your enervated, pointless rage
you cannot otherwise than think
to watch yourself unload
each silent grievance out
upon the vacant waiting page
to dissipate in disappearing ink.

In grief's slant light,
these utterances drop
their heavy cargoes at the wharf,
onto the swarming dock
that groans beneath what time forgot,
unbosoming themselves of all
that excess baggage, all this vast
dendritic dream of life,
the deftly detailed features made
of living's tattered after-image.

In the absence of a dreamer,
scotomas dance upon the retina
to a rhythm audible only
out along the narrow corridors
of unremembered thought, out
among the mirrored swans,
and only from this darkened door.

"Death is just so final,"
she said to me. *"Yes,"* I may
have replied, *"at least
as final as our life."*

V

*My vanity and nostalgia have established an impossible scene.
Perhaps so, I tell myself, but tomorrow I too will have died,
and our times will intermingle and chronology
will be lost in a sphere of symbols.*

—J.L. Borges, *El Hacedor, Dedication to Leopoldo Lugones*

A Note to Hrotsvit

*Hroswitha, playwright, poet and Canoness at the
Imperial Abbey of Gandersheim (935–973)*

How's it going, sister?
God knows it's been a while.
I seem to find, as time goes by,
I'll spend less time than ever
among the weedy monuments
at this far end
of your mostly tidy necropolis,
out here among the pale apostles
of salutary self-torment,
wise forbearance
and happy endings.

Yet, like you I try
to keep my own end up in this
what seems an endless conversation
with the dead, in this
unreciprocated dialog
with you who know not
who I am or was or will be,
with you whose perfect equanimity
leaves room and air enough
for this brash voice of mine,
these mighty shouts, more so than
with any thoughtfully curatorial
assemblage of the living
I can think of.

And just like you, perhaps,
I'm just as glad you have
no clue who really lies
behind this keening rhetoric
I proffer, what sly exempla
harbor here,
what profane comedy.
But like you,
perhaps,
I greatly prize this discourse
with the dark, this intimacy
with the long-departed,
this prospect,
when all is said and done,
of endless happy endings.

Cocktails with the Critic

Princeton, 1953

It was the poetry of reiteration,
a vocal embrace, an administration of aid.
—Leon Edel on Wilson and John Berryman
  from *A Portrait of Edmund Wilson*

1

He stood stock still and motioned me to hush.
We'd stopped under an enormous chestnut
in the heavy damp of the quiet street and listened.
A dog barked twice, maybe two streets over. Behind us,
a volley of hilarity exploded from the row of Eating Clubs
a couple blocks back. We stood immobilized, like prowlers,
while the startled crickets resumed their shrill mechanics.

Across the road, the television news sent silver murmurs
against a lowered window shade while all the other windows
up and down the block exhaled a golden, untroubled aura
of privacy and privilege, standoffish behind their capacious,
firefly-spangled lawns, holding the sidewalk and ourselves,
its prurient pedestrians, firmly, alluringly, at arm's length.

Do you hear it? His eyeglass lenses briefly triplicated
the glow of his unsteady, dancing cigarette. *There it is.*
Do you hear it now? Henry Purcell. Dido's Lament, I think.
And I do believe I might have heard in that dying instant
beneath his husky whisper an inhuman lamentation,
strangely out of place in this bastion of smug suburban ease,
an alto weaving faintly through the falling dark.

2

Hermes to his Orpheus, steering the poet by an elbow,
I tried to steady his lurching step down the upheaved,
root-sundered sidewalk and up to the house where Bunny sat
on his unlit porch to toast the fireflies and greet his guests.
And as he rose to hail our progress on the pitch-black walk,
I distinctly heard the tinkling ice of his highball,
and after a brief exchange, we were bathed in the glow
of an overstuffed, lamplit hospitality, each traveler gathered
from the humid darkness, holding in our thirsty fists
the cool, consoling crystal of an eighteen-year scotch.

The lanky poet had installed himself without ceremony
deep in the nearest club chair, and promptly inquired
after the chances of a refill (My sources tell me
he'd been at it since noon), while our solicitous host
inquired after news of the poet's latest work, which was
the disingenuous purpose of our visit. Seated close
beside him, he watched his lanky, handsome houseguest,
glazed in the purgatorial sweat of the New Jersey summer,
wrestling the recalcitrant clasp of his worn leather folder
to extract a waxwing's nest of typewritten pages scarified
with marginalia and angry strikeouts, at long last
marshalled onto the lengthy linen of his trouser-leg.

We'd barely begun to catch each other up when our host
held out his palm in my direction. Beside him in the adjacent chair
arose a sound that neither of us had likely heard before,
a speaking quite indistinct to begin with, a growling, ancient noise,
bardic, granitic, and now and then distinctly Latinate, Miltonic.
I couldn't make sense of the slurring words at all, just the cadence
of his periods, the wild insistence of my native tongue. He'd
begun an intonation of his *Bradstreet,* the eternal cigarette
dancing gracefully in the air before him, sprinkling bright ash
on the pages of his emphatic, mesmerizing, cauterizing prosody.

3

And that is when it happened. I'd only seen its like once, long ago,
in a smoky Dublin public house, as a young man rose behind me,
a local prodigal recruited to supply the room a ballad dear to all.
After a time, as he spun the old familiar song, another man
approached to stand beside the balladeer and fix his gentle gaze
upon him, and murmur quiet encouragement, offering, from time
to time, an antiphon of whispered prompts and encouragements.

And he took the tenor's elevated hand in his, and held it as he sang.
And the song spun outward for what seemed an eternity,
and all the while the concentration beaded up on that
young singer's brow, and the old man held tight to him,
as if to ballast that anthem's flight, its mortal weightlessness,
its power to carry that boy away, to spirit that voice
away from us, away from all this cumbrous world, for good.

Just so, on that sweltering Jersey night, Wilson very gently
returned the poet's lines to him in an echoing whisper,
as if in affirmation of their haunting melody, confirming
the presence of this rapt little audience in the lamplit room,
encouraging the word-stream, interleaving sporadic distillations
into the syllabic slurry. And then he softly grasped the hand
that waved the cigarette and held it fast, and at that touch,
the poet's voice rang clear again, composed, calmed,
steadied, as if anchored to the living seabed swaying
under the oceanic heave of immemorial rhythms.

4

As we wandered back into the fragrant evening
through the silent streets, all the corner streetlamps
cast their luminescent cones at the empty crossings
as an imperious melody drifted faintly
over the manicured lawns, *verlassen sei auf ewig,*
verlassen sei auf ewig, as if beckoning from the darkness
where fireflies still hovered in the deepest corners,
their glaucous lanterns rising like tiny glowing zeppelins,
only to wink out and tumble earthward at the extremity
of their atmospheres, as if tethered to the earth
by a relentless gravitation securing us to this world,
drawing the gigantic night down into community,
into the consoling company of strangers,
drawing us all ineluctably back to soil.

His Treason

Tea-time with Maclean

That word! As if designed
to thrill the bowel, strike terror,
inspire dread. That word
occurred in my thoughts almost never
throughout my own brilliant career,
and those who count us
wallowed in shame, disillusioned,
living a convenient lie,
barely buying time,
are greatly in error.

The mysteries of motivation
are simple. Simple hatred, don't you know,
will do just fine. Hatred
of the smug, the snugly settled,
hatred of the facile *Gemütlichkeit*
and its innumerable
received wisdoms, contempt
for the pompous populist,
the pusillanimous certainties
of your Average Joe.

Lamplighters clearly knew
exactly what they were looking for
in my time: children
of privilege and prestige,
not idealists, really, but like all true
enthusiasts of sport, those
with a nose for the furtive, the craven,
the bourgeois swaddled in his smug composure,
those with eyes to spot the empty suit,
the easy marks just asking for it:
humiliation, scandal, the awkward
consequences of exposure.

On any Sunday,
we cheer the enemies
of our enemies and rejoice
in the latter's providential humiliation.
And I was amply paid in real time,
so you'd do well to spare me now
the brightly medaled suit,
the fat expense account,
the vapid gestures of your gratitude.

I saw the world, and lived and loved
to see the downfall of my kind.

Gertrude to Her Chambermaid

Come fetch me out my bracelets, girl,
and find that garnet brooch he sent last week,
the heavy piece of twisted silver wire that joins
two rampant red-eyed dragons at my throat.
Be quick about it now, for this could really be
the night, the night he kneels before his queen
no longer just another ardent subject, merely,
but as eager, randy suitor.

(The randier the better, I might add,
since it's been quite the while, dear girl,
since I have couched hot manhood here,
within this royal locket, Object of Desire.)

The old king's energies were quickly spent
those long years gone, I fear,
when once the longed-for scion tumbled
puling into this wretched North of ours
to weave his tiny irksome discontentments
through the salty air out here at Elsinore.

And it's that brooding man-child
that concerns me now, the issue of our youth,
who mopes along the crenelated parapets
and indistinctly mumbles to himself.
The child he was seemed always underfoot,
and I who hauled his rasping pediatric whine
around the place for years, his unrelenting
vice-grip fingers clutching at my skirt,
would just as soon be quit of that
beseeching look of his and play the girl again.

But how he stalks the corridors, that ghoulish
prince of ours! He really needs a woman's touch,
I'd say, and not by God that bloodless wraith,
Polonius' kid, herself as loopy as this brainsick
son of mine: but no, a nice plump Jewish girl perhaps,
who's good at soups and good enough at sex
to pry apart the tiny digits of that mad prehensile
mind of his, relax its grip, and quietly unknit
this tiresome fixation that he's got
on the timely disappearance of my ex.

Wrong Address

following a break-in where nothing was taken

Mingus flipped the kitchen switch,
flooding the room with light, just as,
seeking purchase in the slippery sink,
I tumbled through the unlocked window.

He was after beer. I was after
electronics mostly, firearms, jewelry, cash.
I'd thought the house was empty,
they'd been so quiet. Handing me a Bud,
he led me down the darkened corridor
into a smoky, murmuring, mood-lit parlor,
and proffering a well-stocked humidor,
introduced me to the room.

No one really heard his courtesies at all,
over the Ellington, the Dolphy and the Palestrina,
but there I'd swear stood Henry Miller
hunkered deep in hot exchange and *fratrasie*
with Roscoe Mitchell, V.S. Naipaul (and,
as I recall, some ancient anorexic ballerina),
while Malcom Lowry, peering in at them,
lingered out behind the jalousie.

I can't remember every one of them,
those figures huddled close in little groups, yet
I'd wager Messiaen was one, whistling woodnotes
to a rapt Agrippa, with Tu Fu looking on,
as Arthur Rimbaud traded Yiddish lullabies
with Francis Picabia and a gaunt François Villon,
while in the shadows, in a brass-buttoned blazer,
Old Bill Occam stood alongside Maugham
and Sweeny Todd, and grimly thumbed his razor.

I chugged my brew in haste, and made
a quiet exit past the countless rows
of Anasazi vessels, Inuit soapstone,
Inuit serpentine, and tumbling headlong down
an endless stair, no stereo in sight, no Tiffany
or Fabergé, no sign of car-keys anywhere,
I made my way across an endless sea
of Central Asian weavings, and at long last
issued panicked into the soft gigantic night,
disgorged into its consoling, liberating air.

I'll need to reflect now how I ever wound up
in that improvident place, devoid of value
to those of my profession, and take good care,
my next time out, to preselect a household
somewhat comprehensible, at best some cozy
little sanctum of amply stocked domestic bliss,
chock full of articles at least prehensible, replete
with furnishings I might determine fenceable.

The Majordomo and the Kibbutznik

1. Majordomo

I never once had second thoughts.
I was always grateful for the gig. At fourteen,
I was your youngest hose-puller, awestruck
from my first day on this grand estate, smitten
with the deep herbaceous borders, the towering
Yew hedges, the climbing rose, the trellised Wisteria
and wandering Clematis, the vernal exuberance
of endless Hydrangea lined up like sentinels
along the fragrant, curving drive.

At seventeen, I was your youngest crew boss,
confident in my fastidious husbandry of the exotic
conifers, the sturdy oaks and stately sycamores,
of the kitchen garden's steady succession of plantings
and harvestings, of the stately prospects giving out
from the house in three directions. "Think of all this,"
you said to me a few years further on, "as your own.
I give you free reign." And I'll admit, throughout
the seasons, you've been true to your word.

But nearing sixty now, struggling to please a bed
of fractious Peonies or clear the Horsetail
from a cluster of Daylily, and vaguely overhearing
your voluble, generous words drifting across the lawn,
informing the morning's visitors that "Oscar deserves
all the credit here," I find myself too often distracted,
these days, dreaming of the little patch of ground
behind our own modest house in town,
and wondering how the light, this time of afternoon,
must strike my Foxglove underneath the willows.

And so I fear I may no longer be giving good weight.
I fear that, sometime back, I lost the capacity
to really "own" this magnificent garden of yours,
as I thought I did in youth, my youth in service
to this imperious mistress, this grand estate,
and am called to account now by a modest summons,
beckoned from the convenient fiction
of servile "ownership" into the modest space
of home where each dear thing defies all claim
to owning, where in the searing midday heat,
distractions call me from that shaded place,
our home, where all our scant belongings
cry belonging.

2. Kibbutznik

I was often plagued by second thoughts.
At nine, I thought I knew what I wanted,
and I wanted out. Child of an *Aliyah,* I followed
you, my young parents, into your devotion
to life in these fragile gatherings at Galilee
and the Jezreel, to their spartan labor and danger
and camaraderie. On my table, this photograph
of the four of us in its frame, nut-brown and smiling
on our little doorstep all those years ago,
gives testament.

Here, always in my view, it testifies
to a time of terror and resilience
and happy tasks and well-earned callouses,
and to the sweetness of the corn and melons,
freshly harvested, eaten at those long tables
at sunset, after the day's backbreaking labor,
an image of pungency never to be recaptured.
But still I always imagined another kind
of happiness for myself, yearnings
for the open range, perhaps, or a life
among the bustling boulevards,
mistress of my own agenda.

So when opportunity knocked, at twenty-two,
I married the boy from Haifa and left behind
the shady groves of citrus and avocado,
the sibilant corn-fields, the freezing sentry-duty
under our blanketing stars, and entered the lists
of appreciating value: container gardens
on a half-dozen balconies in town, herbs
and herbaceous borders laid to brighten a dreary
suburban back garden, the odd allotment
at the far end of the shady street. And once again,
before too long, I wanted out.

You are all long gone now, my dear ones,
mother, father, my trusting, heavy-browed
warrior-brother, but you'll be happy to know
that I now know again the flavor of fresh-picked
melons, cucumbers and corn, dead on my feet
after the day's exertions, back in the place
where you brought me long ago to learn of work
and devotion, where I now find myself mistress
of all the fields that feed this little enterprise
in Galilee.

VI

. . . it make no difference where me born, because there is Babylon everywhere.

—Bob Marley

Twilight of the Idols

It wasn't might or beauty made
the ancient city great not
those majestic miles of snaking parapet
the graceful porticoes the lofty
palace galleries and date-lined boulevards
the fragrant groves and massive braziers
blazing at the temple door
but the rummage
of her teeming streets the chaos
at her vast capacious heart.

Not from might alone nor beauty
did this everlasting fame arise
but from the smoking turmoil
of the marketplace the keening lamentations
of her captives in the unresponsive night
the noise that exiled bondage sent
in gutturals and ululating semitones
that issued from a thousand thousand alien throats
discharged into the anxious Mesopotamian sky
released to drift across the dawning city's
sparkling domes and slender spires.

It wasn't really might that made
her redolent name immortal
but that strange susceptibility she had
for differences and the abject fact
of her peculiar genius for change
her hunger to be altered
by the voices that her vast dominion
gathered knit and never synthesized
her willingness to be transformed
by each new trophy of pitiless conquest
and her evident delight in that wanton
cacophony of tongues.

And it was neither loss
of might nor faded beauty brought
those happy blood-drenched epochs to a close
that brought the ancient city to its knees
but the notion some conceived
that they alone were heirs
to greatness by virtue of their kind
and the patrimony of their authorizing myths
and that all the motley polychrome
of alien skins and barbarous tongues
had been allowed by indolence to triumph
at the price of empire's proper selfhood
as if the warring centuries themselves
conspired to breed this barbarous prolixity
that time had cast a pale ironic eye on all
their sanctioned hagiographies
and in the end made mockery of glory
made incremental conquerors instead
of all these infestations of the polity
the impudent presence
of all those hoards of subjugated souls.

It wasn't Ishtar's holy anger only
at the dereliction of the temple grounds
or the shameful tangle of the unkempt avenues
that engendered her demise
but a brute conviction in the populace
that the time had come at last
to see their upstart captives herded off
into an unabated legacy of dreams
and thereby silence difference for good
and make the adversaries quail once more
and reassert the nation's rightful blood
and find their native soil restored
and see their storied Babylon its gods
its rightful masters all its ill-used men
made once more great again.

The Familiar

1

It's hard to remember a time without him,
when that bouncing top-knot wasn't busy
about the house, scouring our brazen goblets
at the well, or at awkward play with my siblings
in the courtyard, tossing this way and that.
Like a young camel's tuft, his jet-black ringlets
quivered, as I picture him, in histrionic rage
at some stubborn shopkeeper in the market.

I'd found myself grown fond of this old slave,
beetle-browed, onyx-eyed, near to my own age,
but the passage of time has frosted that unruly
raven mop now, endearing as the graying muzzle
of a trusted hound, veteran of countless chases,
who luxuriates in the courtyard shade most days,
indolent, dreaming a dream of thirsty gazelles
pausing warily in the streambeds.

I observed him once, from behind a column
in the market square. (In truth, I enjoyed his company,
walking to the town center and back, me on some
official duty, he to provision the household.)

. . . I observed him once in the marketplace,
haggling, wildly gesticulating, until at last
the adversary millet merchant or chickpea vendor,
shoulders hunched, palms up,
quit the field, yielding to the onslaught,
caving to my man's bargain.
(He'd always had a nose for advantage
and a tireless commitment to us, his masters.)

And one day I'd left him to the shops
while I sought news of doings in the Palace.
That day, I recall, the news was not good.
My colleagues at the Ministry of Granaries
were full of foreboding, whispering their dread
of the season's intempestive floods, the obvious
displeasure of Marduk and Ishtar, our deities,
unhappy with the undisciplined priests,
unsettled by the subtle Persians among us,
by our dissolute court, impatient with the rise
of "academies" among the slaves, seated
in their clamorous companies,
disputing their laws,
intoning their barbaric genealogies.

My friends bemoaned those desertions
in the ranks of our armies.
Some said packs of jackals had been spotted
pacing among the rushes by the rivers,
and wolves are often seen now, I've heard,
prowling the deserted mansions
at the outskirts of the of the city.

2

One morning soon thereafter he was gone.
I knew that he had a name, this slave,
the name that he was called among his people,
but we just called him *wardum,* the summons
employed for all his kind in households such as ours.

Yet he had another name, he must have,
I am certain of it, because from time to time,
at evening, I'd overhear the strains of chatter
through the lattice-window of my study. Drifting
from the captives-house across the courtyard,
I'd catch the jangling melody
of their inelegant Aramaic,
that heavy-throated, honking sound,
like the squabbling of cranes in the tall trees.
His name was spoken in that homely cacophony,
the name this slave was called among his people,
I am certain.

And he was a disputatious fellow, that's for sure.
I once had to apply the bastinado
to head and shoulders
in the high street just to save him
from a crueler fate, to extricate him
from an angry mob, and protect my investment.
He sulked all the way home
and didn't speak for a month.

But now he's gone,
and I might have informed the authorities,
but I did not. To what purpose?
My friends at the ministry
say they've watched as long lines of refugees
stream from the city now,
out through the hanging gardens,
out past their sedentary kinsmen,
past the *geonim* who will remain, out past
the derelict Western Gate,

headed downstream, down-valley,
between the waters, into the barrens,
across the shrinking borders of the empire,
headed toward the impossibly distant sea.

He often spoke of the sea on our walks into town,
yammering in those rude gutturals of an element
he had never known, ancient landscapes
that, I imagine, had to figure large
in the narratives he wildly disputed,
those sultry evenings, among his people.

3

Behind these shuttered windows now,
through which the flickering light
of fires set each night across
this unquiet city disturbs my peace,
I see him still.

Sometimes I imagine him
among his own, in motion,
vaguely westward, in some small group,
committed to an uncertain direction,
toward the westward dream,
into an even less certain destination,
guided only
by stories.

11.8.2016

We woke to the smell of blood
in the air, acrid as burning metal.
All the houses went blind
at both ends of the windless street.

Not knowing just what to do next,
we sat very still and pictured
how we'd need to sit this way
four long years or more and saw
all the long knives unsheathed,
and we barely breathed.

We suddenly realized we'd lost
all appetite for lively conversation,
for the juicy ribeye, the discount
coupon, the Theater of the Absurd,
and just as quickly lost all patience
with grim recrimination, smug punditry,
the numberless etiologies
of our exquisite disaster.

And only now we might just may
have learned, after all these years perhaps,
to truly own this engineered collapse,
this determined, systematic retreat
from dignity, and from all we thought
we wanted here, as our own doing,
one way or another, as the unspoken
collusions of a universal negligence.

And maybe now, each one of us
can claim this authorship in earnest
to embrace the insane, insomniac
vigilance that life demands, that society
requires, should life's logic be a logic

of diversity and inclusion—unless,
unless perhaps this dream we dream
is all just wild delusion.

VII
Translations

*He picked up his harp and sang
the word "undr," which means "Wonder."
In his chords I recognized
my own verses . . . I picked up the harp
and sang to a different word.*

—JL Borges, *Undr*

De deserto clamavi: An Introduction to the Translations

In the brilliant wreckage of their voices

*Time's passage led you sorrowing
into shadowed wood, abandoned
on the trackless sand, forlorn
among the smoking ruins of desire,
adrift upon love's vacant heaving sea,
where fiery indirection made
its cogent case for hopelessness,
delirium, and all the uninstructed
music of your hapless poetry.*

*This vagrancy of song is not
some cunning place where meaning lies,
since sorrow only speaks its simple truth,
no ground that holds you fast beneath
a hopeful sky, no steadfast here and now
or changeless somewhere else, no stationary
place you might take bearings from*

*where present time can keep
the past at bay, where all your futures
harbor possibility, where you might
simply choose what song to sing, but where
it's only ever wonder, only ever loss
that sings on cue, and tuneful sorrow
always chooses you.*

After Hanagid, His *Ruined Citadel*

Shmu'el Hanagid, Andalusian Hebrew poet (993—1056)

I barracked my mighty battalions for the night
amid these remnants of a former glory,
this crumbling ribcage of an ancient citadel
ransacked by the armies of the past.

My men now seize uneasy sleep
upon its spine and flanks while I lie wide awake
on a nearby hill, gazing down upon the endless
smoking fires, wondering of the former tenants of this place
whose moldered bodies make a mattress for my men.

Where, I whisper to my heart, are they all now?
Where can they have gone, those prodigious
armies of the past, the teeming townsfolk,
the builders and destroyers, the gaudy nobility
and scraping beggars of this city, and all its slaves
and masters? Where have all the mothers gone,
and the swaying lines of mourners, and the fathers
and the sons, the bridegrooms and the bereft?
And where are those who lived on after these,
down through the generations?

Each one of them dwelt first upon the earth
and now dwell deep within it, passing from palace
to grave, transported from all their pleasant courtyards
into dust. And were they all at once to rise up
from this sleep, they'd lay waste to all our lives
and pleasures. For in fact, my soul, this is indeed what lies
in store for me, for me and all my men besides.

After Moshe Ibn Ezra

Andalusian Hebrew poet (1055–after 1138)

Sing me now your song again, jongleur,
for all these melodies consign my griefs to shadow.
And watching as you play, I marvel at the way
your instrument appears to spring as if
from living bone and sinew, so tightly cleaves
the 'oud's convexity to all its clever minstrel's transports
and his slender swaying curvature.

My heart is spellbound by its many courses.
While some you set to vibrate, others
rest in stillness. And I can only marvel
at the flying plectrum's swift traverse,
the way it, keeping time, will deftly pounce
upon a string and promptly set it free
to throb upon the air, while all your graceful form
enacts the undulations of the song, as if by some
occult concordance of melody and gesture,
some mystic numerology that's shared
between what's seen and what is heard,
we're drawn into the wondrous algebras
made manifest in your performance, the melodies
whose gladness winds about the wounded soul,
caresses like a rippling breeze that whispers
over the face of the deep, shuts tight the doors
of darkness, and opens up to us, your acolytes,
the very mansions of heaven, that we might ascend,
without benefit of any stair, into the blessed realm
of souls and make our way right then and there
away from here, across the rivers of delight.

And hearing you, your hearers' purest thoughts
radiate so clear that witnesses might even say
the angels of the Lord have cast their spirit down
upon us here, for we afflicted are drawn to join
in joyousness these adepts of the lute and pipe,
in whose company we seek sweet respite
from our weeping. And yet, and yet,
my own laments persist in spite of these delights,
my grief for all those father's sons who've perished
from the earth, and all those other souls beside,
companions driven into exile far and wide.

Francesco Petrarca: Or che 'l ciel e la terra e 'l vento tace

At this hour when sky and earth and wind are still,
When all the birds and beasts are caught in sleep,
As night rolls out her starry cart upon its curving track
And the sea rests waveless in its bed,

I lie awake in thought, aflame, in tears, for her image
Lingers in this sweet distress of mine where war is now
Our status quo, this exorbitance of anger and of pain,
And only thoughts of her can bring us peace again.

Thus, from a single living, limpid spring flows everything,
The sweet and bitter both, the font of all my nourishment;
All injury and healing issues from this cruel selfsame hand.

And because my shipwrecked selfhood never finds the shore,
I die a thousand times each day and am a thousand
Times reborn, so far from me, so distant, lies salvation.

Francesco Petrarca: I dolci colli ov'io lasciai me stesso

Those gentle hills wherein I parted from myself,
Those places left behind I cannot ever seem to leave,
Still linger in my sight to freight these hours with all
That Love bestowed, the happy injury I carry everywhere.

How often do I marvel at myself, at this capacity of mine
To blunder on, and haven't managed yet to cast aside
The pleasant yolk of torment that I've tried in vain to shed;
The further on I press, it seems, more tightly grips its grasp.

Like the buck who, wounded by an arrow, harbors in his
Headlong flight the venomed blade embedded in his marrow,
And fleeing ever faster suffers ever greater pain, such

Is my own sad lot these days, where lodged beneath my breast
Love's dire dart brings joy as it drains my life. Stumbling onward,
Racked with pain, at every step this heart grows wearier of flight.

Francesco Petrarca: Gli occhi di ch'io parlai sí caldamente

The eyes of which that I so warmly spoke,
The arms, the hands, the feet, the face
That had so severed me from self, have made
Of me a creature wholly unlike other folk.

Those shining ringlets of a purest gold,
The lightning from that bright seraphic smile
That fashioned on this earth a paradise,
Are now reduced to dust and nothing feel.

Yet here I linger, quickened in my agony and rage,
Divested of the guiding lamp I'd held so dear, adrift
Within the howling storm, abandoned in a shattered wood.

Thus let me now of amorous singing make an end,
For the blood supply of clever composition's all dried up;
My zither's now been tuned for no song but lament.

Francesco Petrarca: Ite, rime dolente, al duro sasso

Go, sorrowing rhymes, descend into the adamant rock
Where hidden in the earth my dearest treasure rests.
Call to her there; she'll answer from the skies,
Although her mortal part so deep in earthy darkness lies.

Tell her now that I've grown weary of this life, weary
Of this cleaving through the fearful seas, but gathering up
The scattered laurel boughs she left below, how I chose
To follow always close behind her, step by sorrowing step,

Lost in this stumbling reverie that's blind to all but who
She was in life, and is in death, and lingers living still in songs
By which the world might contemplate and come to love her.

Ask that she keep watch for my own impending passage,
For surely soon we'll meet again, and ask that she, among
The stars, call out as I approach, and calling draw me to her.

After Francisco De Quevedo

*Persevera en la exâgeracion de su afecto amoroso,
y en el exceso de su padecer*

Silently, within the cloistered alcoves of the soul,
The ravenous wound lies crouched in shadow,
Consuming all my substance as it stokes this confluence
Of flame that sluices through my veins and marrows.

A burning thirst devours my so-called life, consumes
This life of yearning beggared by desire, reduced to ash,
To the incinerated aftermath of that once-bright fire
That gutters now in swirling smoke and darkness.

Retired from the company of men, my daylight hours
Harbor only horror now, while darkest lamentations rise
From clamoring sorrow into the boundless world,
To scatter over life's insensate ocean cloaked as song.
Wallowed in this shipwreck of confusion, I find myself
Transformed, my very heart become a ghastly realm of fright.

Maurice Scève: Le Jour Passé De Ta Doulce Presence

Délie, Dizain 129

That time long past in your sweet company
That offered me a beacon through the winter's dark,
Now only proves your absence to my seeing soul,
And sheds an even darker light than inky night,
A greater burden to this body even than this life itself,
And an ever-present heaviness that drives me to forsake it.
So that, ever since the instant of your disappearance,
Like the wary rabbit huddled in his tunneled room, I cock
My ear to each unsettling sound, confounded in the howling
Company of shades, entombed in deep Egyptian gloom.

After Paul Valéry, His *Palme*

Barely softening the shock
Of his terrifying grace
An angel sets upon my table
The tender bread, the level milk;
With the twitch of an eyelid
He summons prayer to my sight:
—Calm now, calm, just stay calm!
Consider the weight of the palm,
Bowed low in ponderous profusion!

While it sags beneath the gift
Of its abundance, its shape
Is a perfection, its burdensome fruits
Suffice to establish its connection.
Marvel how she quivers,
Like the unhurried filament
That subdivides the instants
And separates without mystery
The beckoning, come-hither earth
From the ponderous sky.

This lovely, swaying arbiter
Of shadow and sunlight
Emblems in the mind
A Sybille's wisdom,
A sybilline slumber.
Anchored to the spot,
The luxuriant waving palm will never weary
Of its greetings and farewells . . .
How noble she is, how tender!
How worthy, as she awaits the touch
Of nothing but the hand of gods.

She murmurs forth a shimmering gold
That rings upon the simple finger
Of the air, and with her silken armoury
Electrifies the desert's soul.
She casts her undying voice
Out upon the sand-filled breezes
That strip and scatter her seed,
Serving as an oracle unto herself,
And glorying in that miracle
That sorrows sing themselves.

Upright in her diffidence
Between sand and sky,
Her fragrant nectars concentrate
With every shining day
Through durations marked
By heaven's clock alone, by a time
That does not count the days
But slowly coalesce
Within her hidden liquors
Every heady fragrance of desire.

Should you find yourself despairing,
Should the stern authority you revere
Spring forth despite your weeping
Just and only here, and nowhere else
But in this languorous shade,
Do not find this perspicacious tree at fault
Who serves you up such hoarded gold
And such authority, that through
Her solemn sap a hope eternal
Rises into ripeness.

For these empty-seeming days,
Lost in the wide universe,
All send thirsty root-hairs down
To labor through the desert floor.
Her heavy hypogean locks,
These proud patricians of the dark,
Never tire in their plumbing explorations
Downward through the bowels of the earth
To find those deepest aquifers
That feed such heights as hers.

Patience, patience, have patience,
Since rooted here
Beneath the azure of these skies
Each atom of its silence bears
The possibility of ripened fruit!
And the happy happenstance will soon arise:
Be it dove or breeze, or the gentlest
Rustling sound, the shape
Of a woman bending down; any one
Of these might just as surely bring that rain
That brings us to our knees.

And should all at once
The proud world's rectitude collapse
In climax, Palm! . . . irresistibly!
Just leave it be to rest upon the dust
To writhe upon the fruits of sky!
And rest assured you haven't squandered
All those hours, should you rise weightless
In the wake of such sweet abandon,
Weightless as the thinker
Whose spirit wastes itself
In such accumulation,
In the nurture of the gifts he's given.

After Yves Bonnefoy, *Aux Arbres*

You who stood aside as she passed by,
Closing ranks behind her passing, you,
Impassive guarantors that Douve, though dead,
Might, being nothing, still be weightless light.

You, leafy prodigies of fiber and density,
Stood right here beside me when she tumbled
Into the vessel of the dead and closed her lips
Upon the obolus of hunger, cold and silence.

Through you I hear the conversation she engages
With the baying dogs, with the misshapen ferryman,
And am yours by virtue of her determined stride,
Defiant through the lengthy night and flooding tide.

A rumbling thunder rolls above your canopy,
And sets the match to our midsummer revelry:
Signs that she has bound her destiny to mine
Through the ministrations of your stark austerity.

After Eugenio Montale, *Meriggiare*

Noontime Walk

To haul your mid-day grief and pallor out
to walk beside a burning garden wall,
to listen as, through plum and thorn,
the blackbirds shriek and rustling serpents crawl.

Through furrowed dirt and tangled vetch,
filaments of fire-ants march across the ground,
their long lines breaking here and there, and see
them tumble headlong from some tiny mound.

To hear between these leaves the distant
palpitations of the scaly sea while, from
the barren peaks, the strident choirs
of shrill cicadas thrum.

And wandering out beneath the blazing sun,
to sadly marvel how your entire life is one
whose every work entails this very act, alas,
to follow the meanders of a wall that's crowned
with pointed shards of broken glass.

About the Author

Born in California in 1951, raised in Japan and Mexico, DB Jonas trained as a classical musician in his childhood and took up the study of Middle Eastern stringed instruments and the music of Europe's Roma as a youth. After several *Wanderjahre* in Spain, France, North Africa, and Italy following secondary school, he studied literature and continental philosophy at the Universities of California and Padova, later earning advanced degrees in Near Eastern Studies and Comparative Literature at Princeton and Yale.

Interrupting a doctoral dissertation on Proust, Nietzsche, and Levinas to pursue an employment opportunity in industry, he never returned to academics. Instead, he became increasingly captivated by the development of complex engineered systems and the study of complex dynamics in natural phenomena. He moved to New Mexico in 1999, where he managed a succession of business operations primarily concerned with the environmental remediation of nuclear and radiochemical facilities. Retiring to his orchards in the Sangre de Cristo Mountains of northern New Mexico, he has returned to his earliest avocations in art history, music, and poetry.

Mr. Jonas has been a finalist for the Riddled with Arrows *Ars Poetica Award*, nominated for a number of *Pushcart* and *Best of the Net* prizes, and has been widely published in journals throughout the US, Canada, Great Britain, Ireland, Holland, France, Romania, Australia, and Israel. His first poetry collection, *Tarantula Season and Other Poems,* was published by Finishing Line Press in 2023. Along with his wife Julie and their dogs, he tends his orchards and gardens surrounded by the manifold inspirations of the Mountain Southwest.

Further examples of his work are accessible at:
jonaspoetry.com

www.ingramcontent.com/pod-product-compliance
Lightning Source LLC
Chambersburg PA
CBHW022013160426
43197CB00007B/415